Dividend Growth Investing

How to Build Future Income Streams Using Dividend Aristocrats

Preface

Unlock the power of dividend growth investing for a lifetime of wealth!

Are you ready to take control of your financial future?

Imagine a world where your investments work tirelessly for you, generating a steady flow of income and growing your wealth, even while you sleep. With the volatility of markets and the unpredictability of economies, securing your financial independence has never been more important. It's not a question of *if*, but **when** you'll need the resilience and stability that only a well-structured dividend growth investment strategy can provide.

Imagine achieving financial freedom and providing for your loved ones with ease. This book is the key to unlocking that reality, guiding you through the turbulent waters of investing with confidence and expertise.

Table of Contents

Introduction

This book is not just about finance but a practical path to financial independence and security. Picture a strategy where your hard-earned money works tirelessly for you, steadily growing over time without the anxiety of constantly monitoring the market. That's the transformative power of dividend growth investing, and within these pages, you'll find everything you need to master it.

What truly sets this book apart is its commitment to accessibility. Most of the time, financial literature can feel like a labyrinth of jargon and complex theories, leaving many aspiring investors feeling lost. However, this book takes a refreshingly different approach. Here, complex financial concepts are dissected and presented in a manner that's understandable and engaging. Whether you're a newcomer to investing or a seasoned pro seeking to refine your strategy, you'll find immense value in its approachable tone.

This book also emphasizes practical application. You'll discover various actionable methods and step-by-step instructions for building a solid dividend portfolio. From selecting the right stocks to managing risk and maximizing returns, every aspect of the process is laid out in clear, easy-to-follow detail.

No matter where you find yourself on your financial journey, this book gives you the power to take control of your future. Say goodbye to uncertainty and welcome a newfound sense of confidence as you harness the power of dividends to create lasting wealth. Whether you dream of retiring comfortably, funding your child's education, or achieving financial peace of mind, dividend growth investing can be your indispensable companion on the path to success.

With the help of this book, you have the chance to thrive in today's dynamic market landscape. Unlock the potential of your investments and pave the way to a brighter and financially stable future with the help of dividend investments.

Chapter 1:

Understanding Dividend Growth Investing

Dividend growth is an investment strategy that earns you a part of the profits of the company in which you are investing. These profit shares are called dividends, and the strategy usually involves reinvesting the dividends in the same company or another dividend growth business to increase your returns over time.

In many ways, dividend growth investing is like nurturing a forest. Imagine you and your friends planted a tree and cared for it (investing in stocks). After some time, you will get fruits which you will share (dividends). You will use the seeds from the fruit to plant new trees (reinvestment), and eventually, you will get even more fruits (compounding dividends). Alternatively, you can sell those fruits for immediate gains (using the dividends for other purposes).

Historical Performance and Advantages

Your dividends depend on the company you have chosen for investment. Not every tree grows fruits, and not every company makes profits. Its financial history should be carefully considered. You need to look for a company with a history of stable earnings, strong cash flow, and a commitment to returning capital to shareholders through dividends. Ideally, you should go for a company with a track record of increasing dividends.

Regarding the history of dividend growth investing itself, you are in for a treat. Many capable investors have seen their earnings grow exponentially in the long run. This strategy isn't for short-term investment. Even if you have chosen the right company for investment, it may not make a profit every dividend period (quarterly or annually).

However, if its growth chart shows a general increase in profits, you can keep reinvesting whatever dividends you get, so that you will earn even more in the long run. The most popular benefits of dividend growth investing include:

- **Outperformance of Dividend-Paying Stocks:** Research has shown that dividend-paying stocks, especially those that continuously grow their dividends, have outperformed non-dividend-paying stocks over the long term. History has consistently demonstrated this trend.

- **Total Return:** Dividend growth investing not only provides you with a stream of income through dividends but also offers the potential for capital appreciation. Reinvesting dividends can enhance your total returns over time through compounding.

- **Resilience During Market Volatility:** Dividend-paying stocks with a history of increasing dividends haven't usually been affected by market downturns. This steady income from dividends can provide a cushion during periods of volatility, and the losses faced in your other investments won't hurt much.

- **Inflation Hedge:** Dividend growth investing is considered a hedge (protection) against inflation. Companies that raise their dividends tend to have pricing power. They can stabilize (or even increase) their profits during inflation by passing on the increased costs to consumers. This way, your dividends will rarely see a decline.

- **Stable (or Growing) Income:** If you are looking for a reliable stream of income, dividend growth investing can be the perfect option. Your growing stream of dividends can supplement your other sources of income, like pensions or retirement savings, providing long-term financial stability.

- **Long-Term Performance:** While it may not always outperform other investment strategies in the short term, its long-term performance has been consistently excellent. Two main variables are on the rise in dividend growth investing - compounding and dividend growth. Unless the company suffers a major loss, you will earn greater dividends in the long run.

Dividend Aristocrats

In the historical sense, an aristocrat is an elite noble or a privileged person. In finance, Dividend Aristocrats refers to elite, privileged companies that consistently pay out increasing dividends to their shareholders. In essence, they have the resources and the product that reels in new customers every year (or quarter) and keeps their existing customers coming back for more.

Companies like AT&T and Walgreens are a part of the Dividend Aristocrats index.

Specifically, this elite index includes companies that:

- Are in the S&P 500 (Standard and Poor's).
- Have a track record of giving out increasing dividends for at least 25 consecutive years.

Significance of Dividend Aristocrats in Dividend Growth Investing

- **Selection Criteria:** It's not easy for companies to be featured in the S&P 500 index. Apart from having a more than a year-old initial public offering (IPO), most of the company's shares should be purchased by the public (not by other businesses or investors), and they should have a high market cap.

  Additionally, increasing the dividend payout every single year for more than 25 years is even more difficult. The company should only use its profits to share the dividends. Paying out from other sources like savings or loans doesn't count. These stringent criteria reflect a company's ability to generate consistent earnings and cash flow growth over an extended period.

- **Track Record of Dividend Growth:** Dividend Aristocrats are known for their long track record of increasing dividends, which demonstrates their commitment to returning capital to shareholders and their confidence in future earnings growth. You can utilize this consistent dividend growth if you are looking for income-oriented, reliable sources of income.

- **Sector Diversity:** The companies in the index come from various sectors of the economy, ranging from consumer staples and industrials to healthcare and utilities. This sector diversity helps reduce risk and exposes your investments to different segments of the market. If one sector is at a market risk, you will have many other options to choose from.

- **Financial Strength:** The Aristocrats have strong balance sheets, stable cash flows, and resilient business models. They often operate in mature industries with predictable revenue streams, doling out consistent returns to its shareholders. This also helps them sustain and grow dividends during economic downturns.

- **Performance:** Did you know records dating back half a century show regular returns to

Dividend Aristocrats investors? Nearly 70% of the dividends came from reinvestments. They have historically outperformed the broader market over the long term. Their consistent dividend growth and stable business fundamentals contribute to their strong performance.

While the Dividend Aristocrats are renowned for their reliability and stability, they are not immune to market downturns or economic challenges. You should still conduct thorough research and consider factors like valuation and competitive positioning before investing in individual companies.

- **Valuation:** It is the process of determining the current or potential worth of an asset, company, or investment opportunity. It helps you assess whether an asset is overvalued, undervalued, or fairly valued and if it can be considered a decent investment opportunity.

- **Competitive Positioning:** This refers to how a company or a product is perceived relative to its competitors in the marketplace. It involves understanding and determining something unique about the company that sets it apart from others in the same industry. You will have to study the industry in great depth to define the competitive positioning of the company you are investing in.

Common Misconceptions about Dividend Investing

Dividend growth is far from a new concept. It is as old as joint-stock companies that originated way back in the 1600s. Nevertheless, many absurd rumors and misconceptions about this steady-income strategy have been doing the rounds of the investment world.

- **Misconception 1: High Dividend Yield Equals Better Investment**

  Dividend yield is an important metric in dividend growth investment. It is a financial ratio that indicates the annual dividend income earned relative to the price of the investment. For example, if a company pays an annual dividend of $2 per share and its stock is trading at $50 per share, the dividend yield would be 4% (divide the annual dividend by the stock trading amount to calculate the percentage). It means you will receive $4 for every $100 invested in stocks.

It may seem like a defining metric where a high dividend yield automatically translates to a superior investment. However, it could be a sign of financial distress or an unsustainable payout ratio. It is possible that a company may artificially inflate its dividend yield by depressing its stock price, which could signal underlying issues within its structure.

Ideally, you should focus on the sustainability of dividends instead of just the yield. A company with a moderate dividend yield but a history of consistent and growing dividends may offer better long-term prospects than one with a high but unsustainable yield.

- **Misconception 2: Dividend Stocks Are Low-Risk Investments**

Dividend stocks are often perceived as low-risk investments due to their regular income streams. However, this perception oversimplifies the risk associated with dividend investing. While established dividend-paying companies may offer stability, they are not immune to market fluctuations or industry-specific challenges.

It is possible you may overlook the inherent risks of dividend investing, like exposure to sector-specific risks or company-specific factors. For example, a company operating in a declining industry may struggle to maintain its dividend payments over the long term, posing a risk if you are relying solely on them for income.

Additionally, dividend stocks are still subject to market risk and can experience price volatility, especially during overly damaging economic downturns or extended periods of market uncertainty. You should assess the overall risk-return profile of dividend stocks in your portfolio and diversify across different asset classes to reduce the risk effectively.

- **Misconception 3: Dividend Investing Is Only for Income Seekers**
While dividend investing is commonly associated with a steady income, it offers benefits beyond just regular cash flow. Dividend-paying stocks can play a crucial role in total return investing, where you aim to generate returns through both capital appreciation (increase in stock value) and dividend income.

With dividend reinvestment plans (DRIPs), you can reinvest dividends automatically to purchase additional shares of the company's stock. Compounding will organically take care of itself, and you will receive greater returns in the long run without doing anything whatsoever.

Dividends can also act as a signal of a company's financial health and management's confidence in future prospects. Companies that consistently pay and grow their dividends demonstrate financial discipline and shareholder-friendly policies. It implies that its stock price will keep on increasing in the long run, so you can simply buy its stocks and sell them at a later date for a profit.

- **Misconception 4: Dividend Cuts Are Always Bad News**

Dividend cuts are viewed negatively by investors in general, as they can indicate financial distress or deteriorating business fundamentals. While dividend cuts can indeed be a cause for concern, they are not always indicative of a company's long-term viability.

In some cases, companies may reduce or suspend dividends temporarily to preserve cash during challenging economic conditions or to fund growth initiatives. While this may result in short-term disappointment for you, it can be a beneficial decision for the company's financial health and sustainability.

You should differentiate between temporary dividend cuts driven by external factors and those arising from deeper operational or financial issues within the company. Conducting thorough research and assessing the company's specific metrics can help you make informed decisions and navigate through periods of dividend uncertainty.

- **Misconception 5: Dividend Investing Is Passive**

Dividend investing is often perceived as a passive strategy, where you buy dividend-paying stocks and collect regular income without active involvement. This passivity may not always generate the kind of income you are looking for. To get a substantial dividend, you need to be more actively involved in the process.

Along with those misconceptions, there are other factors you need to keep in mind. You'll learn more about the following three later on:

1. **Dividend History:** A company's dividend history is the track record of its dividend payments over time. It provides valuable insights into the company's dividend policy, financial performance, and commitment to returning capital to shareholders.

2. **Payout Ratio:** This is a financial metric that indicates the proportion of earnings paid out to shareholders in the form of dividends. A high payout ratio shows the company is in pristine financial condition.

3. **Free Cash Flow:** It represents the cash that a company has available for distribution to investors, debt reduction, or reinvestment back into the business. The higher the free cash flow, the better the company's prospects.

A good investor should also consider the company's long-term growth prospects, including the industry trends, its position in the market, revenue, expansion plans, etc. Monitoring changes in company fundamentals, industry dynamics, and macroeconomic trends is essential to identify potential risks and opportunities within a dividend portfolio.

Chapter 2:

The Fundamentals of Dividend Aristocrats

In this chapter, you'll learn everything you need to know about dividend aristocrats, the eligibility criteria of these companies, and why they are highly sought-after by investors. This chapter explores how dividend aristocrats distribute and maintain increasing dividends, as well as the pros and cons of investing in these companies. You'll understand why stable dividend-paying companies are, their different policies, and the importance of investing in companies that ensure consistent dividend growth. You'll also find two case studies of successful dividend aristocrats.

What Are Dividend Aristocrats?

Launched in 2005, dividend aristocrats are companies listed in an exclusive index in the S&P 500. This index contains a limited number of high-performance, large-cap stocks and is generally perceived as an attractive investment opportunity as it features several stable stocks with promising growth potentials.

There are ETFs, or exchange-traded funds, that allow investors to invest their money in a single package of several companies within the Dividend Aristocrats index. This is a great opportunity for investors who wish to reap rewards by diversifying their portfolios while investing in large-cap stocks. As you can guess from the name, these companies pay consistent dividends to their shareholders, but what makes them different from any other dividend-paying company is that they have a track record of annual increases in their payouts.

The Eligibility Criteria for Dividend Aristocrats

To be considered a dividend aristocrat, a company must be able to maintain that increase for at least 25 consecutive years, meaning that they have solid financials, are characterized by stable business models, and can generally hold up well against economic downturns. Other more stringent factors relevant to the company's liquidity and size are also taken into account when determining a company's eligibility.

For instance, companies must maintain a market capitalization of over $3 billion and sustain a $5 million in daily share trade value for three consecutive months before being listed. While dividend aristocrats don't necessarily offer a high growth potential as compared to other companies, investing in them offers a stable stream of income, making them great for income-focused investors or those who wish to diversify their portfolios.

The stringent eligibility criteria are mainly established to ensure that the index remains exclusive and attractive for potential investors. Since the criteria are very difficult to achieve, and the companies that make it to the index are ones that are giants in their field, the turnover rate among dividend aristocrats remains low. The list is updated annually based on the performance of all companies relative to the requirements. However, listed companies rarely lose their status, and new companies struggle to make it into the index. Those listed within the index perceive their position as a symbol of excellence and prominence.

How Companies Distribute and Maintain Increasing Dividends

To increase their dividend yields every year, these companies must focus on maintaining stable business environments and operations. They also usually offer recession-proof or low price elasticity products. This means that the target consumer segment finds their products essential and that their demand for them remains relatively stable even in the face of economic downturns or price increases. At a time during which other companies might be struggling due to nationwide or even international crises such as COVID-19, dividend aristocrats remain resilient, sustain profits, and keep paying appreciating dividends.

As of March 2024, there are 66 dividend aristocrats spanning numerous sectors, including healthcare, consumer staples, construction, retail, and oil and gas. Walgreens Boots Alliance Inc., Franklin Resources, Inc., Amcor Plc, and Realty Income Corp. are among the highest-performing dividend aristocrats in 2024. Due to the demanding qualifications, there are often fewer than 100 dividend aristocrats at a time.

Startup companies, even those that experience rapid growth and expansion, rarely pay dividends to investors. Management teams usually reinvest profits back into the company to encourage further growth and innovation. This strategy fuels and sustains their ability to grow faster and higher than other startups. Startups with weak business models may incur net losses, preventing them from paying dividends to investors.

Companies with predictable flows of profits, which are mostly large and well-established, are those that pay better dividends. They prioritize paying shareholders, partially to maintain investors' confidence and reward their shareholders, even when they don't necessarily experience regular and consistent growth or rising stock prices. They also have the financial stability and cash flow needed to pay stakeholders consistently either way.

The Pros and Cons of Investing in Dividend Aristocrats

Being able to issue dividends that increase consistently over several years is a sign that the company has solid and sound financials. However, when choosing one to invest in, you should be mindful of their capital allocation. Dividends are paid from the business' profits, which means that whatever is paid to the shareholders isn't reinvested in the firm. If a company is paying its shareholders a very large portion of its profits, it could mean that it's not reinvesting much in its growth. This would put it at a competitive disadvantage, affecting its ability to sustain its high dividend pay and even risk its obsolescence in the long run.

To make sure that the companies you're interested in aren't turning a blind eye to growth opportunities, conduct industry research and competitive analysis, and stay on top of relevant market and technological updates. Another important detail to consider is the reason behind the attractive dividends they're offering. Some companies increase their payout to appease worried investors when the stock value hasn't been appreciating for a while. In the case of dividend aristocrats, which have successfully maintained their ability to issue increasing dividends for over two decades, they likely engage in growth opportunities to be able to fund their payouts while successfully conducting business.

What Are Stable Dividend-Paying Companies?

Stable dividend-paying companies are those able to sustain steady dividend payouts for a given time frame regardless of the market conditions. That said, the amount of issued dividends depends on the company's earnings and performance. The business' rate of the increase in dividends aligns with its long-term profits. Companies that maintain stable dividend policies usually pay their dividends on a quarterly basis in line with their quarterly profits.

Some companies issue their dividends semi-annually or annually, which is also in alignment with their profits for the same period. This policy is among the most popular and least risky for investors because the payout doesn't reflect the company's performance and the market's volatility. Stakeholders are certain that regardless of what happens, they'll still receive a dividend payment, at least on an annual basis.

The board of directors decides on whether they'll reward stockholders through stock shares or cash payments, the amount of capital allocated to dividend payouts, and when to give out these payments. One of their most critical decisions is determining the dividend payment they'll follow. They must decide between retaining, reinvesting, or redistributing the profits.

Aside from investing in growth opportunities for the firm, the board of directors might choose to retain the profits for a number of reasons, including tax liabilities, flotation costs, or future earnings. The board of directors must also account for investors' preferences when deciding on a type of policy to implement. When determining whether to offer stock repurchase options or cash as a reward to shareholders, they should be mindful of the country's tax policies. Once their goals and the respective policies are decided, they use them as blueprints for creating strategic plans to attract investments and establish a competitive advantage in financial markets.

Stable Dividend-Paying Policies

There are generally one of three ways to go when implementing the Stable Dividend Policy. The first is to offer a constant payout ratio, which applies when a company distributes a certain percentage of its profits as dividends to shareholders. This is preferred by several companies as it makes it easier for the board to determine the amount of earnings to retain.

The second option is to implement a constant dividend per share policy, where the company distributes a fixed amount of money as dividends. This allows the company to create a reserve from which they can still pay out dividends even when they incur losses or low profits. This policy is better suited for companies with a relatively stable stream of earnings over several years.

The last option is to combine both policies. In addition to regularly distributing fixed amounts of dividends, this option allows companies to distribute an extra dividend in accordance with their earnings in a given period of time. This option leaves room for flexibility and is great for companies with fluctuating earnings.

The Importance of Consistent Dividend Growth

Many investors have an aversion toward dividend aristocrats. There is a common misconception that it's a boring, low-return venture to invest your money in, as compared to other more thrilling, high-return opportunities. Small-cap companies, especially ones that are high-flying or demonstrate exceptional rapid growth, are undeniably very exciting investment opportunities. However, dividend aristocrats are less risky, more predictable, and more mature. While this doesn't offer the same adrenaline rush as investing in high-flying companies, the increasing stock price and consistent stream of income will be enough to keep you hooked. Dividend aristocrats portray promising earning potentials.

Learning how to evaluate dividend-paying businesses will allow you to gain insights into ways through which you can maximize your investment returns. Many investors prioritize companies that offer a high percentage of the dividend payout relative to the stock price. However, high dividend yields are not enough to base your investment decisions on.

While they are desirable, extremely high dividend yields as compared to the market don't necessarily mean that the company offers a strong dividend. They could be a sign of a depressed stock price instead. In that case, the company might have to resort to dividend cuts or stop giving out dividends altogether.

When choosing a company to invest in, examining the quality of the company and its management is just as important, if not more so, as considering the dividend yield. Assess the company's dividend history and find out whether it has a track record of increasing dividends. This is especially important for long-term investors who seek stable and reliable streams of income and capital appreciation.

Case Studies of Successful Dividend Aristocrats

Johnson & Johnson

In 1972, Johnson & Johnson used to pay its shareholders an annual dividend of $0.009315 per share. By 2020, the company was able to pay its investors $3.98 per share in dividends. In other words, the company experienced an annual dividend increase of 13.5%. It was able to achieve this by stabilizing its earnings by offering a wide range of highly demanded consumer products, which allowed it to increase its payout ratio over the years.

To put things into perspective, in 1993, the company retained around 65% of its earnings, paying out the rest of its earnings as dividends. Just 27 years later, it paid out over 62% of its earnings as dividends, retaining only around 38%.

Procter & Gamble

As of 2024, Procter & Gamble has successfully paid out dividends for 133 consecutive years, increasing its dividends for an outstanding track record of 67 consecutive years. Not only is it a dividend aristocrat, but the company has earned the title of dividend king as well after having increased its dividends for 50 years in a row. This company's dividend stocks are among the most popular and it's for great reason. Its portfolio showcases a history and a promising future of increasing stock valuation and growth prospects. From 2012 to 2016, P&G had an annual dividend growth rate of 6.6%.

Investing in Dividend Aristocrats might not be the most thrilling investment strategy available, especially for more seasoned investors. However, it proves to be an extremely rewarding investment in the long run. The companies listed in this index must meet stringent requirements to qualify, ensuring stability and unparalleled long-term growth potential. The strategy might seem dull to some, but it's time-tested.

Chapter 3:

Identifying Quality Dividend Stocks

Quality dividend stocks mostly belong to companies with strong fundamentals and sustainable business models. These companies have solid earnings growth prospects, healthy cash flows, manageable debt levels, and a competitive edge in their respective industries. Identifying the quality of dividend stocks is a crucial step for a number of reasons. Assessing the quality of dividend stocks makes it easier for you to know that the companies you invest in have a solid track record of consistently paying dividends, indicating financial stability and strength.

It can also mitigate some of the risks associated with dividend investing. For example, companies with poor financial health or unsustainable dividend payout practices can make dividend cuts or suspensions, leading to a loss of income for investors. Proper research and assessing quality is essential for anyone looking to generate steady income, preserve capital, and achieve long-term financial goals through dividend investing.

Fundamental Analysis Techniques for Evaluating Dividend Stocks

Knowing how to assess dividend stocks keeps you safe from risky investments that could potentially decrease your capital. Spending time and using analysis techniques is the right way before picking a dividend stock to invest in.

Here are some fundamental analysis techniques:

Dividend Yield: Divide the annual dividend payment by the stock price to find the dividend yield. A higher yield indicates either an undervaluation of the stock or a bigger percentage of profits being distributed to shareholders by the company.

Dividend Payout Ratio: Evaluate the dividend payout ratio, which is the proportion of earnings paid out as dividends. A sustainable dividend payout ratio varies by industry, but generally, a ratio below 70% is considered healthy. A percentage above 70% may suggest that the company is distributing too much of its earnings and may not have enough funds for reinvestment or future growth.

Dividend Growth Rate: Examine the historical dividend growth rate to assess the company's consistency in increasing dividend payouts over time. A stable or increasing dividend growth rate indicates financial strength and management's confidence in future earnings.

Free Cash Flow: Dig into the available financial data to find the company's free cash flow. This represents the cash generated after accounting for capital expenditures. Having a strong free cash flow allows the company to better maintain and grow dividend payments, as it has sufficient cash to cover operating expenses, invest in growth opportunities, and distribute dividends to shareholders.

Debt Levels: You also need to assess the company's debt levels and debt-to-equity ratio. If a company has excessive debt, it could strain the company's ability to maintain dividend payments during economic downturns or periods of financial stress.

Industry and Competitive Position: Consider the company's industry dynamics and competitive position. For example, a company in a stable industry and a competitive advantage will more likely generate consistent earnings and sustain dividend payments over the long term than a company running in an unstable industry.

Dividend Sustainability: Look for signs of dividend sustainability, like stable cash flows, manageable debt levels, and a diversified revenue base. Avoid companies with erratic earnings or dividend payout patterns signaling financial instability.

Valuation: The last thing you want to do is to assess the stock's valuation relative to its competitors and historical averages. A dividend stock may be attractive if it is trading at a reasonable valuation with a potential upside for capital appreciation in addition to dividend income.

Key Metrics to Assess Dividend Sustainability and Growth Potential

To check a dividend's sustainability and growth potential, you can use fundamental analysis techniques like checking the dividend yield, growth rate, and payout ratio. The following are some of the metrics you need to keep an eye on:

Earnings Growth: Sustainable dividend payments are typically supported by growing earnings, indicating the company's ability to generate profits to sustain and potentially increase dividends over time. Analyzing historical earnings growth trends and future earnings projections provides insights into the company's financial health and its capacity to maintain dividend payments amid changing market conditions or economic cycles.

Industry Position: Companies operating in stable industries with strong competitive advantages are better positioned to maintain dividends over the long term. Understanding the dynamics of the industry in which a company operates, including factors such as market trends, regulatory environment, and competitive landscape, provides insights into the company's ability to sustain dividend payments amid industry challenges or disruptions.

Management Quality: Competent management teams play a crucial role in determining a company's dividend policy and its commitment to shareholder returns. Assessing management's track record, strategic vision, and capital allocation decisions provides insights into their ability to prioritize dividends while also investing in growth opportunities that enhance shareholder value. Transparent communication with shareholders and a prudent approach to financial management further reinforce confidence in the company's ability to sustain and potentially increase dividends over time.

Sector-Specific Considerations

Different industries have varying characteristics and economic sensitivities that can impact dividend sustainability and growth potential. Here are some sector-specific considerations for dividend investing:

Utilities: Utilities are traditionally known for their stable cash flows and high dividend yields. They provide essential services such as electricity, water, and natural gas, which generate consistent revenue streams. Investors often favor utility stocks for their defensive nature and reliable dividend payments, making them suitable for income-focused portfolios. However, regulatory changes, interest rate fluctuations, and environmental regulations can impact utility companies' profitability and dividend policies.

Consumer Staples: Consumer staples companies manufacture and sell essential products such as food, beverages, household goods, and personal care items. These companies typically exhibit stable demand, even during economic downturns, making them resilient dividend payers. They often prioritize dividend payments and are less sensitive to economic cycles compared to other sectors. However, intense competition, changing consumer preferences, and input cost inflation can affect their profitability and dividend growth potential.

Healthcare: Healthcare companies encompass a broad range of sub-sectors, including pharmaceuticals, biotechnology, medical devices, and healthcare services. Healthcare stocks often offer attractive dividend yields and long-term growth potential, driven by demographic trends and healthcare spending. Investors should consider factors such as regulatory approvals, patent expirations, and reimbursement policies when evaluating dividend-paying healthcare stocks. Additionally, the competitive landscape and innovation pipeline can influence a company's ability to sustain dividends amid industry dynamics.

Financial Services: Financial services companies, including banks, insurance companies, and real estate investment trusts (REITs), are significant dividend payers. These companies generate income from interest, fees, and premiums, which support dividend distributions to shareholders. However, financial stocks can be sensitive to interest rate changes, regulatory developments, and credit risk. Investors should assess factors such as loan quality, capital adequacy, and regulatory compliance when considering financial services stocks for dividend investing.

Telecommunications: Telecommunications companies provide essential communication services, including wireless, wired, and broadband internet. These companies often have predictable revenue streams and high dividend payout ratios due to their stable business models and recurring subscription-based revenue. However, technological advancements, competitive pressures, and regulatory changes can impact telecommunications companies' profitability and dividend sustainability.

Energy: Energy companies, including oil and gas producers, refiners, and integrated energy firms, are significant dividend payers driven by commodity prices and demand dynamics. Energy stocks offer attractive dividend yields but can be volatile due to fluctuations in oil and gas prices, geopolitical risks, and environmental regulations. Investors should consider factors such as reserve quality, production costs, and capital expenditure plans when evaluating energy stocks for dividend investing.

Technology: Technology companies have become increasingly relevant in dividend investing, driven by the sector's growth potential and cash-rich balance sheets. Many technology companies have initiated or increased dividend payments in recent years, reflecting their maturing business models and commitment to returning capital to shareholders. However, technology stocks can be volatile and subject to rapid changes in industry trends, competitive pressures, and innovation cycles.

When investing in dividend-paying stocks, you need to consider sector-specific factors alongside broader economic and market conditions. Diversification across sectors can help mitigate risks and enhance the resilience of a dividend-focused investment portfolio. Additionally, conducting thorough fundamental analysis and staying informed about industry developments can help investors identify high-quality dividend stocks with sustainable payouts and growth potential within specific sectors.

Screening Strategies to Find Promising Dividend Aristocrats

Screening strategies can help investors identify promising dividend aristocrats. Here are some screening criteria and strategies to find these high-quality dividend-paying stocks:

Dividend Growth History: Focus on companies with a track record of consecutive annual dividend increases, typically spanning at least 25 years. Look for companies that are members of well-known dividend aristocrat indexes, such as the S&P 500 Dividend Aristocrats or the Dividend Aristocrats Index maintained by S&P Dow Jones Indices.

Dividend Yield: Set a minimum dividend yield threshold to filter for stocks with attractive dividend yields. While a high dividend yield can be appealing, ensure that it's sustainable and backed by the company's earnings and cash flow. Avoid excessively high yields, as they may signal underlying issues with the company's financial health or future dividend sustainability.

Dividend Payout Ratio: Screen for companies with conservative dividend payout ratios, typically below 60% of earnings. A lower payout ratio indicates that the company retains a significant portion of its earnings for reinvestment or future dividend increases, enhancing dividend sustainability.

Earnings Growth: Look for companies with consistent earnings growth over the long term. Sustainable dividend increases are often supported by growing earnings, indicating that the company has the financial strength to continue raising dividends over time.

Free Cash Flow: Prioritize companies with positive and growing free cash flow, as it provides the financial flexibility to support dividend payments and fund future growth initiatives. Compare free cash flow to dividend payments to ensure that the company has sufficient cash flow to cover its dividend obligations.

Stability and Resilience: Consider companies with stable and resilient business models that can weather economic downturns and industry disruptions. Companies operating in recession-resistant industries or those with diversified revenue streams may be better positioned to maintain consistent dividend payments.

Financial Health: Evaluate the company's balance sheet strength, including debt levels, liquidity, and solvency ratios. Choose companies with manageable debt levels and strong credit ratings, as excessive debt can strain dividend payments and increase financial risk.

Industry and Market Position: Assess the company's competitive position within its industry and its ability to generate sustainable competitive advantages. Look for market leaders with strong brand recognition, pricing power, and barriers to entry, as they are more likely to maintain dividend aristocrat status over the long term.

Management Quality: Consider the quality and track record of the company's management team, including their capital allocation decisions and commitment to shareholder value. Look for companies with shareholder-friendly management teams that prioritize dividends and have a history of prudent financial stewardship.

Valuation: Finally, assess the valuation of potential dividend aristocrats to ensure that you're not overpaying for the stock. While high-quality dividend-paying stocks may command premium valuations, seek opportunities where the stock price offers a reasonable entry point relative to the company's fundamentals and growth prospects.

Chapter 4:

Building a Dividend Growth Portfolio

Investors seeking reliable income, long-term wealth accumulation, and portfolio stability should build a dividend growth portfolio. Dividend growth stocks offer a consistent income stream that increases over time, making them ideal for those looking for steady cash flow without relying solely on selling assets. These portfolios also serve as a hedge against inflation, as companies that consistently raise dividends help investors preserve purchasing power and maintain their standard of living amid rising prices.

Dividend reinvestment in a growth portfolio allows investors to benefit from compounding returns, accelerating the growth of their investment over time. Reinvesting dividends into additional shares of stock, you can harness the power of compounding, which can lead to exponential wealth accumulation. This form of investment promotes discipline and patience, encouraging investors to focus on high-quality companies with sustainable dividend growth potential instead of chasing short-term market trends or speculative stocks.

Portfolio Construction Principles for Dividend Investors

Selecting dividend-paying stocks and constructing a diversified portfolio that maximizes income, capital preservation, and long-term growth potential are the initial steps. Here are key principles and considerations for building a dividend portfolio:

Dividend Yield vs. Dividend Growth

You must strike a balance between dividend yield and dividend growth when selecting stocks for your portfolio. High dividend yield stocks offer immediate income but may have slower growth potential, while stocks with lower initial yields but strong dividend growth rates provide higher income potential over time. When weighing these factors, consider your income needs, risk tolerance, and investment objectives.

Diversification across Sectors and Industries

Diversification is crucial to managing risk in a dividend portfolio. Spread investments across different sectors and industries to reduce exposure to sector-specific risks. Diversification will mitigate the impact of adverse events affecting specific sectors or companies and enhance portfolio stability over the long term.

Quality over Yield

Prioritize quality dividend-paying stocks over those with the highest yield. Focus on companies with strong financial fundamentals, sustainable competitive advantages, and a history of consistent dividend payments and growth. Quality companies are more likely to weather economic downturns and market volatility, maintaining their dividend payments even during challenging times.

Dividend Sustainability and Growth Potential

Assess the sustainability and growth potential of dividend payments when selecting stocks for the portfolio. Analyze key metrics such as dividend payout ratio, free cash flow, earnings growth, and debt levels to evaluate the company's ability to maintain and increase dividends over time. Look for companies with a track record of dividend growth and a commitment to returning capital to shareholders.

Reinvest Dividends for Compounding Growth

Consider reinvesting dividends to take advantage of compounding returns. Reinvesting dividends allows you to purchase additional shares of stock, increasing the ownership stake and potential future income. Over time, the power of compounding can significantly enhance the growth of the portfolio and the income generated from dividends.

Regular Monitoring and Rebalancing

Regularly monitor the portfolio and rebalance as needed to maintain the desired asset allocation and risk profile. Review individual stock holdings for changes in dividend policy, financial performance, and industry dynamics. Make adjustments to the portfolio as necessary to address changes in market conditions or investment objectives.

Consider Tax Implications

Be mindful of the tax implications of dividend income, especially for taxable investment accounts. Qualified dividends may be taxed at a lower rate than ordinary income, while non-qualified dividends are taxed at the investor's marginal tax rate. Consider tax-efficient investment strategies like holding dividend-paying stocks in tax-advantaged accounts to minimize tax liability and maximize after-tax returns.

Regular monitoring and adjustments are necessary as that keeps the portfolio aligned with your financial goals and risk tolerance.

Diversification Strategies to Minimize Risk

Asset Class Diversification

Invest in a mix of asset classes, such as stocks, bonds, cash equivalents, real estate, and commodities. Each asset class has unique risk-return characteristics, and diversifying across them can mitigate the impact of adverse events affecting any single asset class. Bonds, for example, tend to be less volatile than stocks and can provide stability to the portfolio during market downturns.

Sector and Industry Diversification

Spread investments across different sectors and industries to reduce exposure to sector-specific risks. For example, if you invest heavily in technology stocks and that sector experiences a downturn, your portfolio could suffer significant losses. Diversification is how you can avoid falling into that trap.

Geographic Diversification

Invest in companies and assets located in different geographic regions to reduce country-specific risks and currency fluctuations. Economic and political factors can vary significantly from one country to another, impacting investment returns.

Company Size Diversification

Diversify across companies of different sizes, including large-cap, mid-cap, and small-cap stocks. Large-cap stocks are typically more stable and less volatile, while small-cap stocks offer higher growth potential but may be riskier. By diversifying across company sizes, investors can balance risk and return potential within their portfolio.

Investment Style Diversification

Consider diversifying across different investment styles, such as growth, value, and income-oriented strategies. Each investment style performs differently under various market conditions, and diversifying across styles can help reduce portfolio volatility and enhance risk-adjusted returns.

Alternative Investments Diversification

Explore alternative investments, such as hedge funds, private equity, and real assets (e.g., real estate and commodities), to further diversify the portfolio. Alternative investments have low correlations with traditional asset classes like stocks and bonds, providing additional diversification benefits and reducing overall portfolio risk.

Regular Rebalancing

Regularly review and rebalance the portfolio to maintain the desired asset allocation and risk profile. Asset classes and investments may drift from their target allocations over time due to market movements, requiring adjustments to realign the portfolio with the investor's objectives and risk tolerance.

Balancing Yield and Growth Objectives

Balancing yield and growth objectives is a crucial aspect of portfolio management, particularly for dividend investors seeking both income and capital appreciation. Here's how investors can effectively balance these objectives:

Income vs. Capital Appreciation

Income-Oriented Investors: Those primarily focused on income prioritize higher dividend yields to meet their current income needs. They may allocate a larger portion of their portfolio to high-yield dividend stocks or income-producing assets like bonds.

Growth-Oriented Investors: Investors seeking capital appreciation prioritize dividend growth stocks with strong fundamentals and growth potential. They prioritize companies with the ability to reinvest earnings for future growth instead of distributing them as dividends.

Diversification

Balanced Approach: Investors can achieve a balance between yield and growth objectives by diversifying their portfolio across both high-yield and dividend growth stocks. This approach helps mitigate risks associated with concentrating too heavily on either income or growth stocks.

Sector Allocation: Allocate investments across different sectors and industries to balance exposure to both high-yield and growth-oriented sectors. This diversification spreads risk and captures opportunities across various segments of the market.

Reinvestment Strategy

Dividend Reinvestment: Reinvesting dividends into additional shares of dividend-paying stocks can accelerate the growth of the portfolio over time. This strategy is particularly beneficial for growth-oriented investors who prioritize capital appreciation.

Income Generation: Income-oriented investors may choose to use dividends as a source of regular income to meet their living expenses. They may opt for dividend stocks with higher yields and a stable payout history to support their income needs.

Risk Management

Risk Tolerance: Consider individual risk tolerance and investment horizon when balancing yield and growth objectives. Investors with a lower risk tolerance may prioritize income stability, while those with a higher risk tolerance may focus more on capital appreciation.

Volatility Considerations: Growth-oriented stocks, particularly those with lower dividend yields, may exhibit higher volatility. Investors should assess their comfort level with market fluctuations and adjust their portfolio allocation accordingly.

Regular Review and Adjustments

Continuously monitor the portfolio and review performance relative to yield and growth objectives. Make adjustments as necessary to maintain alignment with investment goals, changes in market conditions, and evolving financial needs.

Reinvesting Dividends for Compounded Growth

Reinvesting dividends for compounded growth is a powerful strategy for enhancing long-term returns. Here's how it works and why it's beneficial:

Compounded Growth through Dividend Reinvestment

When investors reinvest dividends, they use the dividends earned from their investments to purchase additional shares of the underlying stock instead of receiving them as cash payouts. This strategy allows them to benefit from the compounding effect, where reinvested dividends generate additional dividends over time, accelerating portfolio growth. Essentially, dividends are reinvested to buy more shares, which in turn generate more dividends, creating a cycle of compounded growth.

Increased Ownership Stake and Income Potential

One significant benefit of reinvesting dividends is that it increases an investor's ownership stake in the company. With each dividend payment used to purchase additional shares, the investor's ownership in the company grows over time. As the number of shares increases, so does the income generated from those shares. This not only provides a source of regular income but also enhances future income potential as the portfolio grows.

Dollar-Cost Averaging Benefits

It is possible for investors to benefit from dollar-cost averaging by reinvesting dividends. Reinvesting dividends at regular intervals helps investors purchase more shares during periods of low price volatility and fewer shares during periods of high price volatility. This strategy helps smooth out the impact of market fluctuations, reducing the average cost per share over time. Dollar-cost averaging can lead to improved overall investment returns, especially during periods of market volatility.

Streamlined Process with DRIPs

Automatic dividend reinvestment programs (DRIPs) offered by many brokerage firms streamline the process of reinvesting dividends. These programs automatically use dividend payments to purchase additional shares of stock, eliminating the need for manual intervention.

DRIPs make it easy for investors to benefit from compounded growth without the hassle of manually reinvesting dividends. Additionally, DRIPs often allow investors to reinvest dividends without incurring transaction fees, making them a cost-effective option for compounded growth.

Long-Term Wealth Accumulation

Reinvesting dividends for compounded growth is particularly effective for investors with a long investment horizon. Over time, the compounded growth from reinvested dividends can significantly enhance the long-term growth potential of the investment portfolio. By harnessing the power of compounding, investors can achieve their financial goals and create a more secure financial future. This strategy is especially beneficial for retirement planning, as it steadily builds wealth while generating a reliable income stream.

Chapter 5

Managing and Monitoring Your Dividend Portfolio

Have you built your desired dividend growth portfolio? You can leave it as is, but that is not recommended. Very few passive investors get good returns. To generate a decent, growing income out of your investment, you need to be an active investor.

Creating your portfolio is the hardest task, in part due to researching the market and implementing complex strategies. Managing and monitoring it is relatively easy, though. Regularly try to answer the following questions:

- How much income is your portfolio going to generate this month/year?
- At what rate are your dividends growing?
- Is your portfolio diversified enough, or are you depending on a particular stock?
- How much risk are you taking with your portfolio?

All you have to do is manage your portfolio based on your answers.

Techniques for Ongoing Portfolio Management

Managing an ongoing dividend investment portfolio is primarily about regularly monitoring it. You only need to adjust it if there are changes in the market or in the company's working. Since Dividend Aristocrats are low risk, you won't usually see many changes over the years, especially not any downturns. The most effective techniques of ongoing portfolio management are:

- **Regular Monitoring:** Keep a close eye on the performance of your portfolio and the dividends it generates. You need to track dividend payments, yields, and any other factors that contribute to its performance at least once a week.

- **Reinvestment:** Reinvest dividends to purchase additional shares of dividend-paying stocks or funds. This can help compound your returns over time, leading to accelerated growth of your portfolio. It can be done quarterly or annually, or whenever you receive the dividends.

- **Diversification:** Monitor your diversified portfolio and continue to invest across sectors, industries, and asset classes if you can. Diversification isn't immune to economic downturns, so switch things up when you think a particular sector is going to be adversely affected.
- **Dividend Reinvestment Plans (DRIPs):** DRIPs are offered by many companies, which automatically reinvest dividends to purchase additional shares, often without commission fees. This can free up your time for portfolio management tasks.
- **Dividend Achievers:** Dividend Aristocrats are the most stable companies to invest in, but don't discount Dividend Achievers. Their stocks are priced lower, and they have a decent track record of increasing dividends for a shorter period. Pick companies that have a 10+ years of a record. You can also go with Dividend Champions, which aren't in the S&P index but have a track record of 25+ years.
- **Yield on Cost (YOC):** Monitor the yield on cost, which is the dividend yield based on your original investment. As dividends grow over

time, the yield on cost increases, providing a higher income stream relative to your initial investment.

- **Review Financial Health:** Regularly assess the financial health of dividend-paying companies in your portfolio. Look at key metrics such as earnings growth, payout ratios, debt levels, and free cash flow to ensure that companies can sustain and potentially grow their dividend payments. This can be done once every month.

- **Stay Updated:** Keep yourself updated about economic trends, industry developments, and changes in the dividend policies of companies in your portfolio. Economic and market conditions can impact dividend payments, so it's essential to stay informed about relevant news and analysis. Watch the financial news every day or subscribe to financial channels on social media.

- **Periodic Review and Rebalancing:** Conduct periodic reviews of your portfolio to assess performance, rebalance asset allocation if necessary, and make adjustments based on changes in your financial goals, risk tolerance, and market conditions.

Evaluating Portfolio Performance and Adjusting Strategies

1. Clearly outline your investment goals and objectives. Consider aspects like generating income, capital appreciation, and wealth preservation. Understanding your goals will help you determine the appropriate benchmarks and metrics for evaluating performance.

2. Collect all relevant information about your dividend portfolio, including the initial investment amount, dates of purchases, dividend payments received, and current value of holdings. Also, gather data on any additional contributions or withdrawals made to the portfolio during the evaluation period.

3. Calculate the total return of your dividend portfolio over a specific period (monthly, quarterly, or annually). Total return includes both capital appreciation (or depreciation) and dividend income. The formula for total return is:

*Total Return = (Ending Value - Beginning Value + Dividends Received) / Beginning Value * 100*

Here, "ending value" is the current value of your investment, and "beginning value" is its initial value.

4. Benchmark your dividend portfolio against relevant market indices or peer group averages. Common benchmarks for dividend portfolios are the S&P 500 Dividend Aristocrats Index and the FTSE High Dividend Yield Index. Compare your portfolio's total return to that of the benchmark to assess its relative performance.

5. Calculate the dividend yield of your portfolio by dividing the total annual dividends received by the current value of the portfolio. Compare the dividend yield to historical levels or industry averages to evaluate whether your portfolio is generating an adequate income stream.

6. Consider the risk-adjusted performance of your dividend portfolio by calculating metrics like the Sharpe ratio or the Sortino ratio. These ratios take into account both returns and volatility, providing a measure of how effectively your

portfolio is delivering returns depending on the level of risk taken. The formulas are a bit complex, but these factors are worth considering.

Sharpe Ratio = (Rp - Rf) / σp

Where "Rp" is the average return of the portfolio or investment, "Rf" is the risk-free rate of return (like the yield on Treasury bills), and "σp" is the standard deviation of the portfolio's returns.

Sortino Ratio = (Rp - MAR) / σd

Where "Rp" is the average return of the portfolio or investment, "MAR" is the minimum acceptable return or target return (often set to zero, assuming no acceptable return is below zero), and "σd" is the downside deviation of the portfolio's returns.

7. Evaluate the sector allocation of your dividend portfolio to guarantee it is well-diversified and aligned with your investment objectives. Assess whether certain sectors are over or underrepresented based on their weight in the market or your target allocation.

8. Track the growth of dividends over time to assess the sustainability and consistency of income generated by your portfolio.

You will need to adjust your strategy only if your evaluation turns up unfavorable results (like a few of your dividends are showing a decline or an uncertainty). It simply involves tweaking the previous steps.

- Reflect on your investment objectives and any changes in your financial situation or priorities. Your goals may have evolved since you initially constructed your dividend portfolio, so ensure your strategy still aligns with them.
- Analyze the performance of your dividend portfolio against your benchmarks and objectives. Identify areas of strength and weakness, and determine whether the portfolio is meeting your expectations in terms of income generation, capital appreciation, risk management, and overall returns.
- Replace or trim underperforming assets and look for opportunities to enhance diversification and risk-adjusted returns.
- Adjust the asset allocation of your dividend portfolio to maintain your desired risk-return

profile and capitalize on emerging opportunities. Rebalance periodically to realign your portfolio with your target allocation, especially if market fluctuations have caused deviations from your original investment plan.

- Consider adding new positions or asset classes (make new investments) to enhance diversification and capture potential sources of income and growth.

- After analyzing the future prospects of your chosen companies, adjust your holdings accordingly to prioritize companies with resilient dividend policies and strong fundamentals.

Tax Considerations

On paper, your dividend returns may seem attractive. However, what you actually receive may greatly differ from the amount you calculated. That happens because of tax deductions.

- **Taxation of Qualified vs. Non-Qualified Dividends:** Dividends can be classified as either qualified or non-qualified. Qualified dividends are taxed at the preferential long-term capital gains tax rates, which are lower than ordinary income tax rates. Non-qualified dividends are taxed at your ordinary income tax rates. To qualify for preferential tax treatment, dividends must meet specific holding period requirements and be paid by U.S. corporations or qualified foreign corporations.

- **Tax Rates:** The tax rate on qualified dividends depends on your taxable income and filing status. Ideally, qualified dividends are taxed at rates ranging from 0% to 20%, depending on your income bracket. Dividends that are not qualified are subject to regular income tax rates, which can reach 37% for individuals with the highest incomes.

- **Impact of Holding Period:** To qualify, dividends must be paid by domestic or qualified foreign corporations and held for a certain period. Generally, this holding period is at least 60 days within a specified window around the ex-dividend date for common stock and 90 days for preferred stock.

- **Tax-Advantaged Accounts:** You can reduce or defer taxes on dividends by holding dividend-paying stocks in tax-advantaged accounts like Individual Retirement Accounts (IRAs), Roth IRAs, or 401(k) plans. Dividends earned within these accounts are either tax-deferred (traditional IRAs and 401(k) plans) or tax-free (Roth IRAs).

- **Foreign Tax:** Dividends received from foreign corporations may be subject to foreign withholding taxes. However, you can often claim a foreign tax credit or deduction on your U.S. tax return to offset these taxes.

- **Qualified Dividend Income Limitations:** High-income taxpayers may be subject to additional limitations on the preferential tax treatment of qualified dividends. These limitations are part of the net investment income tax (NIIT) provisions and apply to taxpayers with modified adjusted gross income (MAGI) above certain thresholds ($200,000 for single filers, $250,000 for married filing jointly).

- **Tax-Loss Harvesting:** You can offset capital gains and dividend income by realizing capital losses in taxable accounts through tax-loss harvesting. By selling investments at a loss, you can reduce your tax liability on dividend income and other capital gains.

You will receive Form 1099-DIV from your brokerage or investment firm, which reports dividend income received during the tax year. Qualified dividends are reported separately from non-qualified dividends on this form, making it easier for you to differentiate between the two.

Long-Term Outlook and Staying Committed to the Strategy

As you might know, dividend stocks have often outperformed non-dividend stocks in the long run. It is very likely they will stay the course in the future. Combining factors like inflation hedge, return potential, diversification, and tax efficiency, you may tweak your strategy a bit, but you will be better off committing to your core strategy for getting long-term benefits.

For instance, if you decide to switch your investment to a company's stock that has recently gained momentum, you cannot be as sure of getting the desired returns in the future. Trends are temporary, but trust can be permanent. Staying invested in a company you trust can give you better dividends over time than investing in a short-term, overly hyped up stock.

Conclusion

You now have a solid roadmap to navigate the complexities of the investment world with confidence and clarity. Throughout the book, you learned about key concepts and strategies essential for success in dividend growth investing.

The first section covered the fundamental principles of dividend growth investing, understanding its power to generate sustainable wealth over time. When implemented correctly, this approach can provide a steady stream of income and allows for the compounding effect to work its magic, gradually building wealth over the long term.

You have also explored the concept of dividend aristocrats (companies that have a proven track record of increasing their dividends for at least 25 consecutive years). These companies are often viewed as stable, reliable investments, making them attractive choices for building a strong dividend portfolio.

You also saw the importance of identifying quality dividend stocks. It's a crucial step as it makes it easier to focus on companies with strong fundamentals, mitigate risks, and enhance the long-term growth potential of your portfolio.

Once you've identified quality dividend stocks, the next step is to construct a diversified dividend growth portfolio. Diversification is key to managing risk and maximizing returns, as it helps spread your investments across different sectors and industries.

However, building a portfolio is just the beginning. It's equally important to actively manage and monitor your investments. Reviewing your portfolio allows you to assess performance, identify any areas of weakness, and make necessary adjustments to stay on track towards your financial goals. Whether it's rebalancing your portfolio, reinvesting dividends, or taking advantage of new investment opportunities, staying actively involved in your investment strategy is essential for long-term success.

Besides putting in your effort and time, you need to maintain a learning mindset. There are countless resources available like reputable financial websites, investment seminars, workshops, and online communities dedicated to dividend growth investing.

Remember that patience and discipline are key. Rome wasn't built in a day, and neither is wealth. Stay focused on your long-term objectives, and trust in the potential of dividend growth investing.

References

Berger, R., & Curry, B. (2023, November 29). What Is Diversification? Forbes Advisor. https://www.forbes.com/advisor/investing/what-is-diversification/

CFI Team. (n.d.-a). Dividend Reinvestment Plan (DRIP). Corporate Finance Institute. https://corporatefinanceinstitute.com/resources/accounting/dividend-reinvestment-plan-drip/

CFI Team. (n.d.-b). Investing in Stocks with Dividends vs Stocks without Dividends. Corporate Finance Institute. https://corporatefinanceinstitute.com/resources/equities/investing-in-stocks-with-dividends-vs-stocks-without-dividends/

CFTe, B. D. M. (2023, September 4). Creating the Best Dividend Stock Screener: 4 Strategies & Criteria. Www.liberatedstocktrader.com. https://www.liberatedstocktrader.com/dividend-stock-screener/

Dividend Aristocrats. (2021). Nasdaq. https://www.nasdaq.com/stocks/investing-lists/dividend-aristocrats

Dong, M. J. B. (n.d.). Core Portfolio Construction Principles. Www.ssga.com. https://www.ssga.com/us/en/intermediary/etfs/insights/core-portfolio-construction-principles

Evaluating Dividend Sustainability And Growth Potential. (n.d.). FasterCapital. https://fastercapital.com/topics/evaluating-dividend-sustainability-and-growth-potential.html/4

Garg, V. (2020, January 11). Total Return Formula. WallStreetMojo. https://www.wallstreetmojo.com/total-return-formula/

Hagargi, V. (2023, November 16). Sharpe Ratio vs Sortino Ratio - Understand the Key Difference. Alice Blue Online. https://aliceblueonline.com/sharpe-ratio-vs-sortino-ratio/

Hayes, A. (2022, July 11). Dividend Aristocrat: Definition, Criteria, Example, Pros and Cons. Investopedia. https://www.investopedia.com/terms/d/dividend-aristocrat.asp

How a Dividend Reinvestment Plan Works. (2023, October 26). Schwab Brokerage. https://www.schwab.com/learn/story/how-dividend-reinvestment-plan-works

How to Build a Dividend Portfolio. (2023, September 15). World of Dividends by Simply Safe Dividends. https://www.simplysafedividends.com/world-of-dividends/posts/2-how-to-build-a-dividend-portfolio

How to Invest in Stocks: Dividend vs Non-Dividend Stocks. (2022, December 27). Skillfine. https://skillfine.com/investing-in-stocks-dividend-vs-non-dividend/

jhunjhunwala, D. (2023, March 23). Why Your Business Needs a Balanced Growth Strategy. Medium. https://medium.com/@dhherajjhunjhunwala/why-your-business-needs-a-balanced-growth-strategy-79aea76705e7

Loo, A. (2023). Dividend Policy. Corporate Finance Institute. https://corporatefinanceinstitute.com/resources/equities/dividend-policy/

Portfolio Monitoring and Management in Private Equity Funds. (n.d.). Indus Valley Partners. https://www.ivp.in/resources/articles/portfolio-monitoring-and-management-in-private-equity-funds/

Procter & Gamble. (n.d.). P&G Declares Quarterly Dividend. https://pginvestor.com/financial-reporting/press-releases/news-details/2024/PG-Declares-Quarterly-Dividend/default.aspx

Reynolds, B. (2024, March 19). Dividend Aristocrats In Focus: Procter & Gamble. Sure Dividend. https://www.suredividend.com/dividend-aristocrats-pg/

Sharma, A. (2023, November 26). A Brief History of Dividends: Why Businesses Share the Wealth. Www.linkedin.com. https://www.linkedin.com/pulse/brief-history-dividends-why-businesses-share-wealth-aditya-sharma-xtvtf?trk=public_post_main-feed-card_reshare_feed-article-content

Stamm, W. (2016, June 6). Procter & Gamble: A Dividend King With 60 Years Of Dividend Increases (Part 4 Of 18). Seeking Alpha. https://seekingalpha.com/article/3980102-procter-and-gamble-dividend-king-60-years-of-dividend-increases-part-4-of-18

Sullivan, P. (2023, July 24). Building an Income Portfolio with Dividends. Www.linkedin.com. https://www.linkedin.com/pulse/building-income-portfolio-dividends-patrick-sullivan-mba

Taube, S. (2024, March 20). The Top 7 Dividend Aristocrats by Yield: March 2024. NerdWallet. https://www.nerdwallet.com/article/investing/top-dividend-aristocrats-list

Tax Considerations in Dividend. (n.d.). FasterCapital. https://fastercapital.com/startup-topic/Tax-Considerations-in-Dividend.html

Team, C. (2023a, October 18). S&P 500 Dividend Aristocrats. Corporate Finance Institute. https://corporatefinanceinstitute.com/resources/equities/sp-500-dividend-aristocrats/

Team, C. (2023b, December 7). Stable Dividend Policy. Corporate Finance Institute. https://corporatefinanceinstitute.com/resources/accounting/stable-dividend-policy/

Team, I. (2022, May 17). The Power Of Dividend Growth. Investopedia. https://www.investopedia.com/articles/basics/04/072304.asp

The Power of Dividends: Past, Present, and Future. (2021, March 5). Hartford Funds. https://www.hartfordfunds.com/insights/market-perspectives/equity/the-power-of-dividends.html

What Is Dividend Growth Investing & How Does It Work? (2022, June 21). Titan. https://www.titan.com/articles/what-is-dividend-growth-investing

Wiley Global Finance. (n.d.). Why Dividends Matter - Fidelity. Www.fidelity.com. https://www.fidelity.com/learning-center/investment-products/stocks/why-dividends-matter